CONTENTS

I beg of you to wage continual warfare against negative moods, and never fail to begin again." Ven. Bruno Lanteri

The Venerable Bruno Lanteri

Spiritual Counsels for Life in the World

Timothy M. Gallagher, O.M.V.

Discerning Hearts
www.discerninghearts.com

ISBN-10: 0988627043
ISBN-13: 978-0988627048

Cover design: Kathleen McGregor

The Venerable Bruno Lanteri and the Lay Vocation

Ven. Bruno Lanteri lived from 1759 to 1830 in Piedmont, the northwestern corner of Italy. In these critical years, the French Revolution spilled violently into Italy, abducting successive pontiffs, Pius VI and Pius VII, and persecuting and pressuring the Church on all levels. During these troubled times, Ven. Lanteri faithfully pursued his chosen works: giving and training others to give the Spiritual Exercises of St. Ignatius of Loyola, forming priests and laity in holiness, disseminating thousands of books for spiritual growth and in defense of the faith, upholding Church teaching against the errors of the day, hearing countless confessions, and guiding many with spiritual direction. His deep life of prayer sustained him in struggles with ill health and in his labors for the Lord. Ven. Lanteri's message of hope and his ceaseless invitation to *begin again* strengthened those who sought his aid and continues to inspire many today.[1]

Twenty years ago, I spoke at a symposium on Ven. Lanteri and the laity.[2] For that event, I gathered quotations from Ven. Lanteri's writings to lay men and women and grouped them around various themes. With

---

[1] For a complete biography of Ven. Lanteri, see *Begin Again: The Life and Spiritual Legacy of Bruno Lanteri*, as shown on the final page of this book.

[2] Sept. 4-8, 1995, Mondo Migliore, Rocca di Papa (Rome). The talk was published in *Lanterianum* 4 (1996): 28-64.

further revision, this book offers these texts to a wider public.[3]

The passages chosen provide a window into Ven. Lanteri's heart: a heart that loved, that reached out to others in human and spiritual friendship, and that, itself filled with faith, rejoiced in the spiritual growth of those it approached. Through his own words and those of witnesses, we will watch Ven. Lanteri interact with laypeople, explore his sense of the dignity of their vocation, listen as he urges laypeople to live with holiness, and ponder the key emphases of his spiritual direction of the laity. It is my hope that these pages will reveal the figure of Ven. Lanteri as a spiritual guide of the laity and that his call to holiness in the lay vocation will resound again today.

The first part of this book centers on basic themes in Ven. Lanteri's spiritual direction of laypeople. In the second, a selection of his letters presents this guidance in practice.

---

[3] These selections first appeared in English in *Lanterianum* 7 (1999): 51-67, and later in *The Venerable Pio Bruno Lanteri and the Lay Vocation* (Boston: Oblates of the Virgin Mary, 2007). All translations are the author's.

I. THEMES OF SPIRITUAL DIRECTION

"THINK OF GOD IN A SPIRIT OF GOODNESS"[4]

Ven. Lanteri desires to lead laypeople to know the goodness of our God and so to relate to him with love and trust.

We must always have before our eyes that saying of the Holy Spirit: "Think of God in a spirit of goodness."[5] Therefore, we should seek to attain sentiments worthy of God, first of all in ourselves, so as to inspire them also in others, and so reach the goal of loving him and bringing all others to love him. (Directory for the Exercises of St. Ignatius, *Un'esperienza*, 249).

He truly fulfilled that which the Holy Spirit says, "Think of God in the spirit of goodness," and he had truly great sentiments in regard to the divine goodness (Loggero, *Positio*, 631).

---

[4] This expression and others like it abound in Ven. Lanteri's writings: "Think of God in a spirit of goodness, not in our own way but in a way worthy of God"; "It will be their familiar practice, their common practice, to speak about God with all, in a way, however, worthy of him. This manner of proceeding accords with the counsel of the Holy Spirit: 'Think of God in a spirit of goodness.' Wisdom 1:1." [5] Wisdom 1:1.

It will be my care always to have that great idea of the majesty and goodness of God that the saints have in heaven (To a Married Woman, *Positio*, 537).

I continually recommend you in prayer to our good God, that he may fill you with graces and blessings (To Leopoldo Ricasoli, *Carteggio*, II, 163).

I will take care not to think of the Divine Majesty as if he were of our condition, that is, that he were weary of so much instability, weakness, and forgetfulness, punishing me, therefore, by removing the help and graces I need…. We do a great wrong to God when we measure him by our own limits. I will always attribute to him that which is proper to him, that which is most precious to him, that is, to be filled with goodness, merciful and compassionate, to be a loving Father who knows our weakness, bears with us and forgives us (To a Married Woman, *Positio*, 538-539).

"EVER MORE COMMITTED TO THE GLORY OF GOD"

Ven. Lanteri encourages laypeople to promote the glory of God through their activity in this world. [5]

And so I wish you every true good, and I take consolation in seeing you ever more committed to the glory of God since there is no greater purpose nor one more consoling in this world (To Leopoldo Ricasoli, *Carteggio*, II, 166).

Allow me to continue to recommend to you in this regard that you take good care of your health, especially by giving at least a part of your tasks to others so as to have, in the course of the week, some moments of peace. Otherwise the bow that is always bent will finally break. And be sure that Christian Friendship has great need of you, such that the greater glory of God also requires this same care for your health (To Ricasoli, ibid, 166).

---

[5] "As irrational creatures glorify God by manifesting the beauty and goodness that God has given them, so man glorifies God by manifesting in his actions the virtues of God, by imitating Jesus" (AOMV, SII, 432, f.29). Personal spiritual notes of Ven. Lanteri.

I congratulate you warmly on the new and important occupation given you in the court of the small King, all the more since in this employment you will find greater opportunities of doing good, especially by means of books. Oh, what a great thing it is and how consoling to serve as an instrument to glorify God (To Ricasoli, ibid, II, 168).

It is opportune now to work toward and assist in the reestablishing of other religious communities as well, both of men and of women, since they are means for promoting the glory of God and the salvation of souls. Think of how much good you will do if you can help in re-establishing them (To Ricasoli, ibid, II, 379).

The Lord has placed you at the head of this work [The Christian Friendship] which is so great for the glory of God, nor have I any doubt of your commitment in furthering the plans of God in this regard (To Ricasoli, ibid., III, 29).

"THESE SACRAMENTS ARE THE CHANNELS"

Ven. Lanteri repeatedly urges those he guides to receive often the sacraments of the Eucharist and Reconciliation. These are the means to obtain the grace necessary to live as faithful disciples of Christ.

I will go to confession and receive communion every eight days as I have done for many years. These sacraments are the channels that God has established to communicate to me his graces and his light. Therefore my perseverance depends upon the faithful practice of them. When I approach these sacraments I will ask insistently of my Lord the help I need to fulfill the obligations of my state, and especially to love and be loved by my husband (To a Married Woman, *Positio*, 535-36).

Add to this a weekly practice of the sacrament of penance, and more than weekly reception of Holy Communion, with the firm and invincible resolution to always begin again and to hope ever more firmly in God. In so doing, I guarantee that you will never fall into grave failings (To Ricasoli, *Carteggio*, II, 161).

You will be especially sure of remaining in the grace of God if you never cease to approach the sacraments weekly and more often if necessary. These are the channels through which the Lord especially chooses to communicate his graces of which, above all, we have need (To Ricasoli, ibid, 170).

"AND THESE ARE PRAYER AND SPIRITUAL READING"

Ven. Lanteri believes firmly in the importance of classic practices of prayer: meditation, spiritual reading, examination of conscience, retreats, and similar exercises. He desires that laypeople do these faithfully in accordance with their lay condition.

For this purpose, he not only did spiritual reading and meditation himself but recommended these holy practices to all, both in private conversations and in hearing confessions, in which he was tireless, as I can witness, having been present and seen this personally (Craveri, *Positio*, 619).

I will be faithful in making fifteen minutes of meditation every day and fifteen minutes of spiritual reading, and the examination of conscience in the evening. I will also attend Mass if I can. It is very right that I give an hour of the day to God when the obligations of my state of life permit it (To a Married Woman, *Positio*, 536).

And you will become an effective instrument all the more if you keep yourself united to God especially by the spiritual practices proposed in the Christian Friendship such as prayer and spiritual reading, together with the practice of the holy sacraments. Oh, how I long for the joy of knowing that you have done these holy exercises (To Ricasoli, *Carteggio*, II, 168).

To have one day of total solitude would help a great deal to restore your energy and the courage so necessary in the service of God, such that, I beg you to observe this practice especially when you are in your summer home where it will be easier yet for you (To Ricasoli, ibid., 258).

Try, further, to add regularly each day a small amount of meditation and spiritual reading, and do not fear that the Lord will not grant all that you desire. Be persuaded that the difficulty in continuing with these practices is more in our minds than in reality, and remember that God merits everything, nor does he allow himself to be outdone in generosity. Perhaps for meditation the book of Fr. Huby could be of help, and for spiritual reading, *The Consolation of the Christian* or else *The Thoughts of Bourdaloue* or *The Sentiments of the Christian*, especially the second volume, if you have not yet read and reread them (To Ricasoli, ibid., II, 400).

Catalogue of books useful for the education and spiritual direction of young women and that can also serve them as a guide for forming a small and suitable library of books, especially on leaving home and entering the world [After this title a list of several hundred books follows, a carefully prepared catalogue providing a solid spiritual formation for young women] (*Carteggio*, III, 51-95).

"THE METHOD FOR THIS PRAYER"[6]

Ven. Lanteri is convinced that prayer is more fruitful and perseverance easier if we build into it a certain order. What is done haphazardly and only by impulse is less likely to endure; hence the importance of a program of prayer.

Because of this I can never recommend enough to you the daily meditation of the holy truths of our religion, made with real commitment, with the heart, and continued with a holy obstinacy, and always, as much as possible, at a fixed hour of the day. It will be easier to maintain this practice if you also do spiritual reading daily with calm reflection and on well-chosen spiritual books (To Ricasoli, ibid, 170).

---

[6] "I propose never to omit my meditation and always to do it with method and fidelity…. With regard to Communion I propose to prepare the evening before the matter of the preparation and of the thanksgiving, to think about this immediately upon awakening, and to do all with method and fidelity." Personal Spiritual Directory of Fr. Lanteri, written when twenty-two years old, *Un'esperienza*, 63-64. Carey writes: "Stronger than on the individual components of Lanteri's regimen of prayer is his insistence upon regularity and perseverance in its practice. The fruits of such a life of prayer are to be seen after long-standing practice, in the gradual perfection of the subject through prayer." John Carey, *The Spiritual Doctrine of the Venerable Father Bruno Lanteri in His Letters of Spiritual Direction to Sir Leopoldo Ricasoli* (typescript, 1993), 55.

I will read this series of spiritual thoughts once a month and on all occasions when I experience something contrary to my wishes or upsetting to me in some manner (To a Married Woman, *Positio,* 540).

Methods of meditation suggested to me by Fr. Lanteri: prepare for myself the matter of meditation; calm my spirit; place myself in the presence of God; propose these truths to myself as worthy of faith, as worthy of love, as able to be practiced or able to be imitated; present this teaching to my memory; convince my intellect of its truth; embrace its practice with my will; look to the past to see how I have put it into practice; to the present to see the means offered to make it easier to practice in the future; resolution to put it into practice. To carry this out I need the help of God, and therefore I will have recourse to him and seek also, in order to obtain this help, the intercession of the Virgin Mary and of the other saints (To Gabriella Solaro della Margarita, *Carteggio,* II, 236, note 6).

Method for spiritual reading: after the choice of a book and after having chosen the time for this reading, begin the reading by raising my heart to God, confident that God himself speaks to us through the book; that it is a letter he sends to us from his heavenly dwelling. Ask of Him an attentive and docile heart, and the grace to understand these truths well so as to profit spiritually by them. Then read with attention and without hurry, pausing on those truths that speak more to our present needs and returning from time to time to our own heart and to the God who is speaking to us. Never finish the reading without some holy resolution (*Carteggio*, II, 284).[7]

I ask your forgiveness for not having sent you as yet the method for prayer I promised you and also a list of books for your spiritual reading and that of the Lady Marquise, your worthy spouse. I do not have time at the moment, and so it will have to be for another time (To Ricasoli, *Carteggio*, II, 157).

---

[7] From a program of spiritual life that Lanteri prepared for a woman not named in the document. Ven. Lanteri also added a method for meditation, essentially that of the three powers of the soul given by St. Ignatius in his Spiritual Exercises.

Ven. Lanteri repeatedly encourages his spiritual directees to an almost "obstinate" perseverance in the exercises of the spiritual life, to resist any temptation to weaken in their practice but rather to continue, day after day, to practice them faithfully. He sees in this fidelity a source of great blessings: "A holy determination in the practice of the ordinary exercises of piety, especially meditation and spiritual reading, will always be a source of great blessing for you" (To Ricasoli, Carteggio, II, 161).

May God be praised for your perseverance in the proposals you made in your time of retreat; they are of the greatest importance. I do not doubt that the Lord will continue to grant this perseverance to you until the end, and I will never cease to beg of him this grace. Continue without fail in your devotions two times a week; be inflexible in never omitting your spiritual reading, meditation, and examination of conscience. Have the goodness to give me word of these often, not only with regard to your fidelity in practicing them, but also of the stirrings of heart that you experience and the books that you use in doing them (To Ricasoli, ibid, 247248).

Give great importance to fidelity in your spiritual practices. Keep yourself from that tacit disregard for them by which one says that it does not matter so much if I do not find time for meditation or spiritual reading or the examination of conscience, etc., whether in order to be with others, or for some task, or out of some physical indisposition (To a Married Woman, *Positio*, 541).

"IT IS IMPOSSIBLE TO HOPE TOO MUCH"

The insistent call to hope is a primary characteristic of Ven. Lanteri's spiritual direction, and it explains in significant part the attraction many felt toward him. He always has a word of comfort for the discouraged, and all who come in contact with him depart with renewed hope.

If we wish to speak of his hope in God, this was the joy and the comfort of his entire life. He would say: "We must always grow in this virtue: it is impossible to hope too much. The one who hopes for everything, obtains everything." Therefore he had from God the grace of comforting the troubled, of providing clarity for those in doubt, of giving joy to the sorrowing, of encouraging the hesitating. He consoled many religious in their sorrows, and penitents departed from his confessional filled with consolation (Ferrero, *Positio*, 603).

Whatever my failings may be, I will never lose heart, aware that I will commit many such failings; but I will always ask God's forgiveness immediately, and strive to do better (To a Married Woman, *Positio*, 538).

And I will be persuaded that discouragement is the greatest obstacle on the way of salvation (Ibid, 539).

And do you not yet see that the enemy seeks by this means to diminish your peace of heart and confidence in God? These two dispositions are so necessary in order to pray well. Therefore, take to heart the counsel of St. Teresa, "Let nothing disturb you," not even your spiritual failings, because these are the object, the basis, and the ground for God's infinite mercy, which infinitely surpasses the malice of all the sins of the world (To Leopolda Martigliengo , *Positio*, 552)

Call to mind from time to time these words of Sacred Scripture: *Behold the Lamb of God* (Jn 1:29); *I have not come to call the righteous, but sinners* (Mt 9:13); *It is not those who are well that have need of the physician, but those who are ill* (Mt 9:12); *If anyone has sinned we have an advocate with the Father* (1Jn 2:1); *The Lord waits to show us His mercy and in forgiving you, He will be exalted* (Is 30:18); *All have sinned and have the need of the glory of God* (Rm 3:23); *There will be greater joy in heaven for a sinner who repents than for ninety-nine just who have no need of repentance* (Lk 15:7).[8] Continue to reflect on the parable of the Prodigal Son, of the Good Shepherd, on the way Jesus on this earth dealt with sinners, and finally on the outpouring of love with which he immolated himself on the cross and does yet every day on the altar, for sinners. Let the conclusion be that we place ourselves immediately in God's presence, recognizing him as Father, hoping in him, never for a

---

[8] Author's translation of scriptural texts from the Latin that Ven. Lanteri uses.

moment doubting that we shall be well received by so good a heavenly Father; that he will generously forgive us; that, indeed, we will be filled with his blessings (Letter to "a discouraged person," not further identified: *Gastaldi*, 170).

I sense in your letter, which I am so happy to have received, a certain discouragement in the service of God. By the grace of God, beware of this. There is no enemy more to be feared than this (To Ricasoli, *Carteggio*, II, 161).

Above all, I recommend to you as insistently as I can, to keep yourself from discouragement, from trouble of heart and sadness. Strive always to keep your poor heart in peace, to encourage your heart, and always to serve God with a holy joy (To Ricasoli, ibid, 170).

"NUNC COEPI" ("NOW I BEGIN")[9]

A further characteristic of Ven. Lanteri's spiritual direction is closely linked to the preceding: the reassurance that, when we fall, nothing is lost and, in fact, we give the Lord a further opportunity to show us mercy. The one important thing is continually to begin again, *confident in the goodness, love, understanding, and inexhaustible patience of our heavenly Father. In his spiritual guidance, Ven. Lanteri never tires of repeating this call to* begin again *in times of failure or discouragement.*

Whatever my shortcomings may be, I will never lose heart. I know that I will commit many, but always I will ask God's forgiveness and will seek to grow. Thus, should I fall even a thousand times a day, a thousand times I will begin again. I will come to know my weakness ever more clearly and, with the same peace of heart, will promise God to strive to grow. I will take care not to think of the Divine Majesty as if He were of our same condition (To a Married Woman, *Positio*, 538).

---

[9] "If I should fail even a thousand times, I will never lose heart, I will never lose peace, but I will always immediately say quietly to my heart, 'Now I Begin.'" Spiritual Directory, *Un'esperienza, 66.* Such phrases abound in Ven. Lanteri's writings. The biblical text in which Ven. Lanteri finds the words "Now I Begin" is Psalm 77:10. See Carey, *The Spiritual Doctrine*, 82-85.

Always aim at these two things, which I advise you to review often with a holy obstinacy: 1. Never consciously to offend God; 2. should you fall into some defect, never to continue to will this but always to raise yourself again with humility and courage, and begin again, confident that you have been truly forgiven by God at the very moment in which, with humility and trust, you ask His forgiveness (To Ricasoli, *Carteggio*, II, 170).

I beg of you the goodness to let me know whether you are persevering in your good interior dispositions, whether you are receiving the sacraments, whether you ever omit the meditation and spiritual reading upon which we agreed when I had the joy of speaking with you. If this should not be the case, I beg you not to lose heart and to begin immediately, since discouragement is the worst of all things (To Ricasoli, ibid, II, 259-260).

Ven. Lanteri exhorts those he directs to have "a great and generous heart" in the service of God, to dedicate themselves with energy to the things of God. Those he guides feel themselves stirred to do more, to undertake new initiatives, to consider new possibilities, encouraged in this by their director.

Generosity of soul, freedom of heart in acting and in suffering, and fidelity in resolutions made to God: this is the quality I will strive to possess (To a Married Woman, *Positio*, 540).

A firm resolution never to commit a mortal sin at whatever cost; on the contrary, I will take constant care never to commit a deliberate venial sin (To a Married Woman, ibid, 534).

I will let no day pass without obtaining some victory over my passions, at times by renouncing my own will, at times by bearing with gentleness of heart the difficult things that occur (To a Married Woman, ibid, 536).

It will be my glory always to profess openly and with freedom my desire to live as a good Christian and to have

God as my King, and not the world with its teachings. By this means, I will overcome human respect, and I will close the door to many evils (To a Married Woman, ibid, 537).

I am sure that you will continue to serve God with a great and generous heart even in the midst of daily failings, all the more because, according to St. Francis de Sales, "Perfection itself does not consist in never failing but in never persevering in the will to fail" (To Ricasoli, *Carteggio*, II, 164).

It is certain that we should never lose sight of the "conquer thyself" of St. Francis Xavier, in order to cooperate with the grace of God. If you practice this with liberty of spirit and a great heart, not becoming anxious about the difficulties that may arise but rather disregarding them, this will not be as difficult as it appears (To Ricasoli, ibid, II, 248).

Above all, I have asked the Lord to give you great courage and firm hope in God, so that by this virtue, overcoming all discouragement and striving not to lose that precious time that the Lord gives us, you may attain greater good for yourself and for others, especially since the Lord has given you so many means for this and the desire to accomplish it (To Ricasoli, ibid, II, 251).

"I WILL CONSIDER THESE AS FAVORS AND OPPORTUNITIES"[10]

Suffering.... No spiritual direction can be complete unless it offers effective counsel in regard to suffering. Ven. Lanteri guides those he directs to look toward the final answer to the question of suffering—the crucified Christ—and to see in such suffering the hand of God that disposes all things for our spiritual progress.

Anxieties, temptations, aridity, heaviness of heart, tribulations, injuries, unpleasant situations, offenses, ingratitude, crosses, matters which do not go well, and sorrows of various kinds: I will expect all these, even from those I love and those I have helped. But I will never consider these as evil nor will I regard their origin in men, but rather in God. I know that nothing can take place against the will of God. I know that this is the way he himself followed here on earth and through which he led the saints closest to him, even his very mother, so as to glorify her correspondingly in heaven. And so I will consider these as favors and opportunities that he gives me, so that I will need to ask his help, so that I will know my weakness, and do penance for my sins. I will try to

---

[10] "Every difficult thing, every sadness of heart, every lack of desire, every obstacle whether internal or external, is an occasion God gives me that I may merit all the more, and I desire to profit from these." Personal spiritual notes of Ven. Lanteri, *Manoscritti*, 1, 17.

accept them, confident that this is the road he has laid out for me, that all is ordered for my good, and that my part is to seek to benefit from these situations (To a Married Woman, *Positio*, 539).

Let us fix the eyes of our faith and love on the crucified Christ, and we will see that he was not satisfied only with the possibility of suffering, but that he truly suffered every kind of pain, both in body and in spirit, since it is not the possibility of suffering but sufferings themselves that cause us to gain merit. Let us then accept from his hand every occasion of suffering and practicing virtue, and since all things are disposed for our salvation, let us try to enter into his purpose of love, to follow his plan the best we can, convinced that grace is linked to all that happens, to every cross, and that every such grace we welcome will receive an eternal recompense and reward (in *Gastaldi*, 473)

"TO BE GENTLE AND LOWLY OF HEART"

Ven. Lanteri contemplates with special joy on the "unshakable gentleness in every occasion" of Christ (Un'esperienza, 146), and the warmth of this humble attitude that is "characteristic of Christ" (ibid, 133). He desires to foster such dispositions in those he guides. Ven. Lanteri finds in our inevitable failings an opportunity to grow in a humility that removes all discouragement regarding such faults and gives us peace.

I will treat all those who live here with great warmth and politeness…. I will be always joyful in the company of others, and I will willingly accede to the tastes of the other women in matters of leisure time and in all that is not a question of sin (To a Married Woman, *Positio*, 535).

Peace of heart, a joyful spirit, love of neighbor, compassion for the sorrows of others, goodness of heart, patience, quiet endurance, affability, acceptance of others' desires that are not of offense to God: in short, to be gentle and lowly of heart. This is the character I propose to have and that I will continually ask of the Sacred Heart of Jesus and of Mary (To a Married Woman, ibid, 540).

I beg you then with all the energy of my heart, not to be afraid of your past failings but rather to let the memory of them lead you to a greater knowledge of yourself and humility before the Lord and, at the same time, to encourage you to trust all the more in our heavenly Father, who is always so ready to welcome, forgive, and assist us (To Ricasoli, *Carteggio*, II, 170).

"THROUGH THE HANDS OF MARY"

Ven. Lanteri invites all to "a tender love of the Virgin Mary" and the confidence in her of children toward their mother (Un'esperienza, 69), convinced that such dispositions open a rich channel of grace. Deeply Marian himself, Ven. Lanteri also reveals his love for Mary in his ministry of spiritual direction.

He loved the Virgin Mary deeply.... He spoke very often about her. He said that it was not enough to inspire devotion to her in people but that it was necessary to lead them to a great confidence in her as well (Loggero, *Positio*, 606).

The Theologian Lanteri professed a special devotion to the Blessed Virgin Mary, the guardian angels, St. Joseph, St. Francis Xavier, Blessed Alphonsus of Ligouri, and the other saints of Paradise, and especially recommended preparing through novenas for the celebration of their feasts; above all, he had great fervor for the Queen of heaven, as is commonly known (Craveri, *Positio*, 623).

I will always profess a special devotion to the Sacred Heart of Jesus and to the Virgin Mary, who are the sources of all graces, and I will direct myself to them in all my needs (To a Married Woman, *Positio*, 536).

And because love for Mary does not wish to remain alone but seeks companions and friends, so with all those he directed spiritually he shared his own fire and warm love, counseling them and proposing to them the works that he himself did, because, as he said, "to bring souls to God we must lead them to pass through the hands of Mary, just as the graces of God all pass through her blessed hands"
(*Gastaldi*, 397).

"GOD HAS PLACED ME IN THIS STATE OF LIFE"

Ven. Lanteri urges all lay men and women to see their lay state of life as their specific path to holiness: it is in "this state ... and in no other" that God wills "that I serve him and gain my salvation." Ven. Lanteri leads these men and women to see their lay state in life as their God-given vocation and to strive to fulfill faithfully the tasks of that state.

The state of life ... in which I find myself is the condition in which I can, I ought, and I desire to become holy. And so I need to see clearly my obligations and the means to fulfill them. My true happiness consists in the faithful practice of these (To a Married Woman, *Positio*, 534).

1. My heart must belong totally to God and to my husband, not only out of natural attraction, but also because of a commitment contracted with God himself. 2. I must make every effort to maintain harmony among all in the house and to seek and to create a domestic peace. 3. I must strive to win the affection of all who live near to us (To a Married Woman, ibid, 534).

I will seek to understand the inclinations of all in the house so as to provide for them, and to please them cheerfully in all that is not of offense to God, even though at times this may cost effort (To a Married Woman, ibid, 535).

God has placed me in this state of life and in no other, so that may I serve him and gain my salvation. All the circumstances and events related to my state in life such as the different temperaments of those with whom I deal, the matters that arise, the times and places in which these things take place, all of this forms the order of providence the Lord has chosen for my salvation (To a Married Woman, ibid, 537).

Counsels given to me verbally by Fr. Lanteri…. To carry out every occupation and temporal matter that may arise as if fulfilling a task given by God, and to consider that the entire day is a mission given to me by God (Gabriella Solaro della Margarita, *Carteggio*, II, 236, note 6).

I am happy that you are free from every other task, since in this way you will better be able to attend to the duties of your state of life and always to promote the glory of God, to find joy in a true inner peace (To Ricasoli, *Carteggio*, II, 198).

"THEY WILL PRAISE GOD ETERNALLY IN HEAVEN"

Ven. Lanteri kindles in others what his own heart feels: a profound and living sense of our eternal destiny, that goal of life expressed in St. Ignatius's Principal and Foundation: "Man is created to praise, reverence, and serve God our Lord, and by this to save his soul" (Spiritual Exercises, 23). The hope of such eternal blessedness gives meaning to the daily life of the Christian.

I am created by God for this single purpose, that is, that I may praise and serve him and, in the end, gain my eternal salvation (To a Married Woman, *Positio*, 534)

At times I find myself in spirit in your Villa at Fiesole, deeply regretting that we cannot be together there again this year as last, [11] since nothing in this world is of such great value as the opportunity to spend several days peacefully occupied with the great matters in life alone: God, the soul, and eternity (To Ricasoli, *Carteggio*, II, 168).

---

[11] Ven. Lanteri recalls the retreat he gave to the "Christian friends" of Florence the year before in Ricasoli's villa in Fiesole, outside Florence.

Allow me to suggest that, instead of the holy Exercises, you make a day of retreat as soon as possible. On that day, setting aside all external occupations, you could make two meditations, one on the purpose of man's life, the other on death. You could read something relevant to these truths and on Christian hope, reviewing during that time the proposals made in your last retreat for the purpose of gaining new courage to undertake their practice (To Ricasoli, ibid, 197).

I warmly congratulate your most illustrious and beloved Lordship and the Lady Countess, your most esteemed wife, that you have become the parents of twins, of little Stanislaus and Maria Julia, two more hearts who will praise God in heaven with their parents and the rest of the family, as I firmly hope in the Lord (To Ricasoli, ibid, II, 345).

II. LETTERS OF SPIRITUAL DIRECTION

Ven. Lanteri composed the following three letters of spiritual direction for a laywoman, Gabriella Solaro della Margarita, mother of Clemente Solara della Margarita, well known in Italian history as a political figure and faithful Catholic. The mother of six children, she is described as a woman "of faithful heart ... with a will constantly inclined toward the good, but somewhat impatient, almost sharp..." (Carteggio II, 234, note 3). *Gabriella was a sincerely Christian woman, whose life brought blessing to many. Translated from Carteggio, II, 208-09.*

My Lady and my Daughter in Jesus Christ,

I just received your esteemed letter, which gave me real joy. I am happy to know of your safe trip and the excellent health of all in your family. I see no reason why you may not entrust your little Louise to your dear sister, the Lady Countess Vidua. She could not be in better hands, and the reasons for doing so are many. In my view, you may do this with total peace of heart.

And it gives me greater happiness still to know that Fr. Ferrero is already there with you. It is important, then, to begin immediately, to arrange with him for receiving Communion, and to do so as often as you can. You must be consistently faithful to meditation and to spiritual reading, if it be only a quarter of an hour of meditation and a single page of spiritual reading, and the same also for the examination of conscience which you can do while you are working. Do not forget to raise your heart frequently, with tenderness and peace, to God, and to make acts of mortification, especially interior ones; for you, this means the effort to live each moment with a gentle and joyful spirit. For the love of God, do not forget to resist constantly a negative frame of mind, and never cease to begin again at all times.

Do not wait until you have devotion to begin all this; begin all the same, without devotion, because devotion will come with time, and these are precisely the means to acquire it. Devotion should be the effect and not the cause of these practices. And for the rest, you know that true devotion consists in readiness to be faithful to the Lord and not in sentiment. I hope that you will soon share consoling news with me in this regard.

I ask you to give my greetings to Father Cesare and to tell him that I would be happy to see him here, and that I always hope to be able one day to visit with him there. For the present, tell Fr. Ferraro that, even though I have not yet had the joy of meeting him, I ask him to give you no rest in committing yourself to practicing all that I have just recommended to you and to call you strictly to account, and I will be grateful to him for this.

I bless you together with all your family, I recommend myself to your prayers, and I am, with the highest esteem and respect,

Your Servant and
Father in Jesus Christ,

Lanteri

Turin, May 22, 1807

In the following letter, Ven. Lanteri seizes a moment from his occupations to send word to Gabriella by her son who was leaving the city to visit her. From Ven. Lanteri's initial remarks, it appears that he has not heard recently from Gabriella. Translated from **Carteggio***, II, 234-36.*

Madame,

I would like to use this opportunity of the departure [from Turin] of Monsieur your son[12] for some profit, but I do not know of what I should speak: Should I praise you for your fidelity to God? Ought I chide you? I do not know at all. So I will take a sure course and that is to counsel you to begin each day, abandoning the past to the Lord's mercy and the future to his divine Providence. In the meantime, reflect each day that you are entrusted with a mission by the good God. In regard to your temporal affairs, never let anything trouble you, and the same with respect to your faults, taking care to counteract them immediately by an act of love of God. Be attentive to practicing the virtues of patience and gentleness; you could make a special examination concerning this in the evening and at midday. Do not forget meditation, at least for a quarter of an hour, frequently raising up your heart to God throughout the day.

Remember spiritual reading as well, even if it is but a single page. Finally, do not omit to receive communion at least two or three times a week. I beg you to inform me about all these things, praying to the good God that he assist you in carrying them out.

It may be that I will come myself to learn how you are doing. It would be a great consolation for me, and I hope for it all the more since my eyes, which continually

---

[12] Gabriella's son Clemente, at this time sixteen years old.

grow weaker, will not permit me to dedicate myself to other occupations that might hinder me from coming, as happened last year.

I do not have time to remain longer with you in this letter as I would desire, and so I conclude by recommending myself to your holy prayers, and blessing you, having the honor of being,

Your Servant and
Father in Jesus Christ
Theologian Bruno Lanteri[14]

Turin, July 4, 1808

In this third letter, Ven. Lanteri has just heard of the death of Enrico, Gabriella's young son, and writes a note of both human and spiritual solace to the grieving mother. Translated from Carteggio, *III, 197-99.*

Madame,

I learned from Madame your mother-in-law of how you have lost your little child Enrico. In one way, as I think of this, I feel deep sorrow for what has happened to you, since no sacrifice could be more painful for you. He had such wonderful qualities that all loved him, and how much more his own mother. And so, because of this, you have every reason to feel his loss and to weep for him.

Yet, in another way, I share with you a joy that you have very surely gained a protector in heaven who cannot fail to care for you from his heart, since he is your son. And because you love him so deeply, turn your thoughts to his eternal happiness, share in his glory, and do not imagine that you have lost him. It would be wrong to think so, since you have lost him only from sight and not in reality. Consider that he is at your side like another angel, that he encourages you to dedicate yourself to the things of heaven and to share in his joy; that he assures you of his efforts before the throne of the Most Holy Trinity on your behalf, as also for his father, his brother, and his dear sisters, to obtain for all of you great and abundant graces for your eternal salvation.

And so, remain in continual and loving conversation with him. Speak to him about all that you experience in your own heart and in your family, and about whatever is of importance to you. Be on guard against thinking that he does not care about you or is powerless to help you, since such thoughts would be to misunderstand the immense love and almost infinite power that each of the Blessed enjoys, with all the other divine perfections that God shares with them in the greatest possible abundance.

And so, if before you had no reason to become discouraged in the service of God, you have much less reason now. I would add that, if it were possible for your little Enrico to feel any sorrow even now in heaven, it would be to see you discouraged and saddened because of him, because of your own failings, or because of the difficulties you meet in the service of God.

This will be the remedy for all your feelings of sadness and any lack of courage: the thought that, with the grace of God and the protection of your little Enrico, you can do all things.

I beg you to share some part of these reflections with your respected and worthy daughters to console them also in their great affliction for the loss of their beloved brother. Tell them that I too take part in their pain and that I will hold them constantly present in the Holy Sacrifice of the Mass to obtain for them consolation of heart and their spiritual growth.

I end this letter by blessing you all, and I am, with all possible esteem and respect,

Your servant and father in Jesus Christ
Theologian Pio Bruno Lanteri

From Bardassano, July 31, 1818

Ven. Lanteri wrote the following two letters to his spiritual son Leopoldo Ricasoli, a dedicated Catholic and father of six. The letters manifest the characteristic emphases of Ven. Lanteri's spiritual direction: a regular practice of the sacraments, faithful daily prayer, determined resistance to discouragement, and the constant readiness to "begin again." Ven. Lanteri penned this first letter when Leopoldo was twenty-six and he himself fifty-five. Translated from Carteggio, *II, 160-61.*

Monsieur and dear friend in Jesus Christ,

I do not wish to let this mail coach depart without writing you a short note in haste. I usually wait for the day the coach leaves to write, and usually some unforeseen occupation impedes me from writing as I planned. That is what happened last week, and that is what is happening again today.

I cannot hide from you the real and heartfelt joy that your most valued and most welcome letter gave me. I awaited it with impatience, and I hope you will renew this pleasure for me weekly if you can, all the more since this is not just a matter of satisfying my wish and my concern in your regard, which certainly are not small, since I can never forget the great goodness you showed me. But this is a question of the glory of God that can be promoted by this means; and so, do not refuse me this joy.

In your letter I sense discouragement in the service of God. For God's sake, guard against this since there is no enemy more to be feared than this. A holy tenacity in the faithful practice of the ordinary exercises of piety, especially in meditation and spiritual reading, will always be a source of great blessings for you. Add to this a weekly practice of the Sacrament of Penance and more than weekly Holy Communion, with a firm and invincible resolution always to begin again, and to hope ever more firmly in God, and I guarantee you safety from major failings, at least from their unhappy consequences that you fear with such reason. It is of these matters especially that I beg you to write and tell me how you find yourself, since the well-being of your soul, which certainly can never be indifferent to me, depends principally on these.

I have no further time to write. I beg you to present my respects to Madame the Marquise, your worthy spouse, to Monsieur and Madame d'Azeglio, and above all to the most worthy Doctor Bucelli. Be assured that I will never forget you in my prayers before God. As I wait to hear once more from you, I recommend myself to your prayers, and I am in haste,

Your Servant and A[mi] C[hrétien][13]
Pio Bruno Lanteri

Turin, February 29, 1804

---

[13] "Christian Friend," that is, a member of the Christian Friendship group founded by Fr. Diessbach and later led by Ven. Lanteri.

In this letter, Ven. Lanteri once more encourages Leopoldo to fidelity in his life of prayer and to a firm hope in God. Translated from Carteggio, *II, 321-22.*

Most Worthy Signor Prior and Amico Cristiano[14] in Jesus Christ,

I was happy to receive your letter and it could not have given me greater consolation. For a long time now, I have kept you in my heart in a special way before the Lord and ardently desired word from you about your situation. May the Lord now be praised, who willed to give me this through your letter, and may he be all the more praised and blessed as I see that this news is good in every respect.

I note, however, that you fear for your constancy and certainly not without some reason in regard to your own part since we can never sufficiently fear and even despair of ourselves, and so are held all the more, for this very reason, to flee occasions and dangers. Yet lest this fear, so just in itself, lead to discouragement and dejection of heart, we must inseparably accompany it with the firmest hope in God, our Father in heaven, who loves us so deeply. He alone can and indeed truly desires to help us and infallibly does help us if we are constant in using the means of grace given us by his fatherly heart for this

---

[14] "Christian Friend": see the preceding note 9 On a separate sheet Gabriella writes: "Counsels given to me by the Abbé Lanteri when we spoke: never become discouraged in those times when I fall, but humble myself, ask forgiveness of God, and begin again, 'Then I said, "Now I begin"' [Ps 77:10], always begin again. Do every occupation, every temporal affair to fulfill a task given by God; consider throughout the whole day that I have been sent to these tasks by God." *Carteggio* II, 236, note 6

purpose. These are a faithful practice of the sacraments, never interrupting this for any reason whatsoever, as well as the constant practice of meditation and spiritual reading, and a frequent exercise of some external mortification.

You know too that all this is not so difficult to manage and that a means that could help you remain firm in this practice would be to send me, from time to time, an account in some detail of both the practice and the fruits of these exercises. In this way I would also have the consolation of contributing, as much as I am able, to your spiritual progress. Do me this favor, my dearly beloved Signor Prior, so that in this my cherished solitude, where I have become as though useless to my neighbor,[15] I may be at least of some spiritual assistance to you. I ask this all the more, since my days will not be long because of my illnesses which, rather than diminish, persist all the more, hastening my departure from this world of sorrow and the union with my gentle Jesus for which I long.

With regard to your children whom I love tenderly, rest assured that I will never forget in prayer before the Lord. I hope firmly in the Lord that he will always bless them and will give you the wisdom necessary to save them from the corruption of the age.

---

[15] In punishment for his clandestine assistance to Pope Pius VII, then a prisoner of Napoleon, the French police ordered Ven. Lanteri to leave Turin and confined him to his country home, effectively suppressing his priestly ministry. This exile lasted three years until the fall of Napoleon in 1814.

And begging you to give my most distinct respects to your worthy spouse and to the Amici, [16] to whose prayers I particularly recommend myself, with the greatest consideration and most cordial friendship and gratitude, I am

Of Your Most Illustrious and Most Esteemed Lordship

Your Most Devoted, Most Indebted and Most
Affectionate
Servant and Friend,
Pio Bruno Lanteri

From my country place, December 10, 1812

---

[16] That is, the "Friends," the members of the Christian Friendship.

PRAYER FOR THE INTERCESSION OF VENERABLE BRUNO LANTERI

O Father, fountain of all life and holiness, you
gave Venerable Bruno Lanteri great faith in
Christ, your Son, a lively hope, and an active
love for the salvation of his brethren.
You made him a prophet of your Word and
a witness to your Mercy. He had a tender
love for Mary, and by his very life he taught
fidelity to the Church.

Father, hear the prayer of your family and, through
the intercession of Venerable Lanteri, grant us the
grace for which we now ask…. May he be raised to
the altars that we may give you greater praise.
We ask this through your Son, Jesus Christ, our Lord.
Amen.

Send requests for prayers and word of favors received to
www.brunolanteri.org

To contact the Oblates of the Virgin Mary, visit
www.omvusa.org

A full biography of Venerable Bruno Lanteri is available
online and through bookstores:

Timothy M. Gallagher, O.M.V., *Begin Again: The Life and
Spiritual Legacy of Bruno Lanteri*, Crossroad, 2013

SOURCES

Carteggio: Paolo Calliari, O.M.V., *Carteggio del Venerabile Padre Pio Bruno Lanteri (1759-1830) fondatore degli Oblati di Maria Vergine,* 5 vols. Turin: Editrice lanteriana, 1976.

Un'esperienza: Timothy Gallagher, O.M.V.,

Un'esperienza dello Spirito. Pio Bruno Lanteri: Il suo carisma nelle sue parole. Cuneo: AGA, 1989.

Gastaldi: Pietro Gastaldi, O.M.V., *Della vita del Servo di Dio Pio Brunone Lanteri fondatore della Congregazione degli Oblati di Maria Vergine.* Turin: Marietti, 1870.

Manoscritti: *Manoscritti del fondatore Pio Brunone Lanteri, 8 vols.* Rome, Centro Stampa O.M.V., 19761980.

Positio: Amadeo Frutaz, *Pinerolien. Beatificationis et CanonizationisServi Dei Pii Brunonis Lanteri Fundatoris Congregationis Oblatorum M. V. (1830). Positio super introductione causae et super virtutibus ex officio compilata.* Rome: Typis Polyglottis Vaticanis, 1945

Made in the USA
Las Vegas, NV
21 July 2023